Give me mercy

Anthology of Wisdom and Inspiration

RAY BEVAN

Unless otherwise stated, Scripture quotations are taken from the Holy Bible, New
International Version, copyright © 1973, 1978, 1984 by the International Bible
Society. All rights reserved.

All correspondence to:
Ray Bevan
The King's Church, 69 Lower Dock Street, Newport, Wales, NP20 1EH
Tel:+44(0)1633 244453
ray.bevan@kings-church.org.uk
www.kings-church.org.uk

Published by Integrity Media Europe
Unit 1 Hargreaves Business Park, Hargreaves Road, Eastbourne, BN23 6QW

ISBN 978-1-907080-04-3

the **DEVOTIONAL RESCUE** series

Give me mercy

Anthology of Wisdom and Inspiration

RAY BEVAN

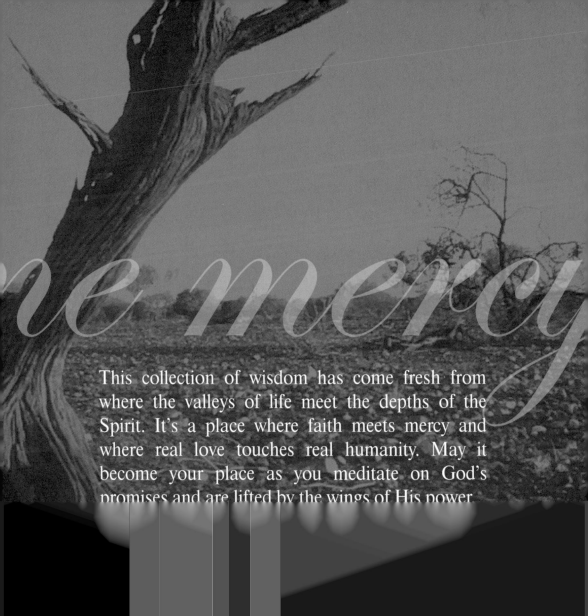

ne mercy

This collection of wisdom has come fresh from where the valleys of life meet the depths of the Spirit. It's a place where faith meets mercy and where real love touches real humanity. May it become your place as you meditate on God's promises and are lifted by the wings of His power.

mercy

wisdom

intimacy

faith

the cornerstones

Mercy disarms the executioners.

"Mercy triumphs over judgement."
James 2:13

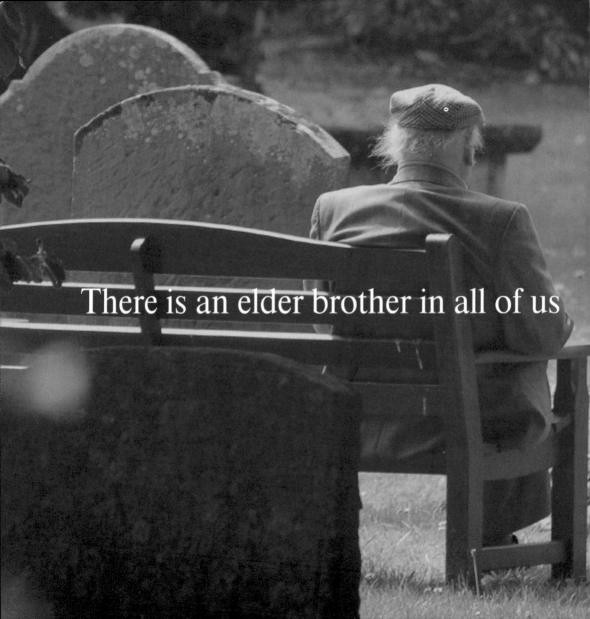

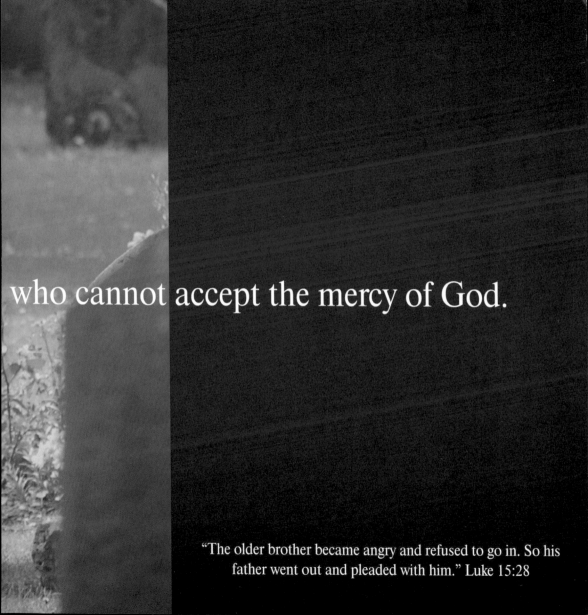

who cannot accept the mercy of God.

"The older brother became angry and refused to go in. So his father went out and pleaded with him." Luke 15:28

Mercy qualifies the disqualified.
It dismantles the gallows.
It dismisses the firing squad.

"...in His great mercy He has given us new birth into a living hope..." 1 Peter 1:3

God builds with what others have rejected.

Failure is a part of the journey. Stop beating yourself up for it.

"We all stumble in many ways…" James 3:2

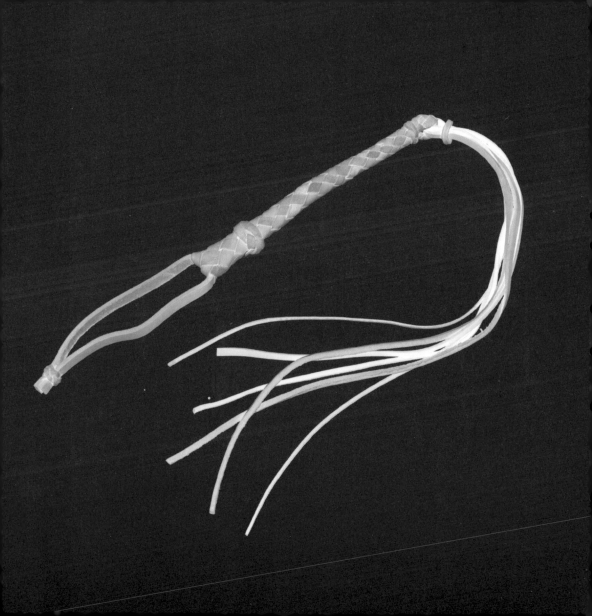

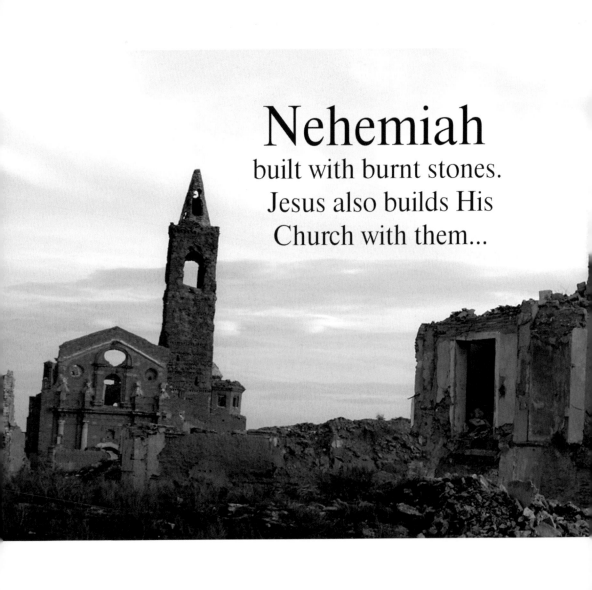

Nehemiah built with burnt stones. Jesus also builds His Church with them...

"…can they bring the stones back to life from those heaps of rubble - burned as they are?"
Nehemiah 4:2

Your failure
doesn't prevent you
from being used again.

"So Jacob was left alone, and a man wrestled with him till daybreak. When the man saw that he could not overpower him, he touched the socket of Jacob's hip so that his hip was wrenched as he wrestled with the man. Then the man said, "Let me go, for it is daybreak." But Jacob replied, "I will not let you go unless you bless me." Genesis 32:24-26

"The LORD said to Moses, "Chisel out two stone tablets like the first ones, and I will write on them the words that were on the first tablets, which you broke." Exodus 34:1

GRACE
MERCY

Grace gives us what we don't deserve.
Mercy stops God giving us what we do deserve.

mercy
wisdom
intimacy
faith

the cornerstones

Jesus is saving
the best till last.

"...everyone brings out the choice wine first
and then the cheaper wine after the guests
have had too much to drink; but you have
saved the best till now." John 2:10

"...then a great and powerful wind tore the mountains apart and shattered the rocks before the LORD, but the LORD was not in the wind. After the wind there was an earthquake, but the LORD was not in the earthquake. After the earthquake came a fire, but the LORD was not in the fire. And after the fire came a gentle whisper." 1 Kings 19:11-12

God is not always in the spectacular

Just because it's mystical

doesn't make it credible.

"The secret things belong to the LORD our God, but the things revealed belong to us and to our children forever, that we may follow all the words of this law."
Deuteronomy 29:29

Be rooted to the past – not rutted to it.

Destiny is not the two letters A and Z. It's an alphabet.

Genesis 45:4-5

Life is
unp
redict
able.

You can't plan for it.
But you can prepare for it.

You can't earn this stuff. It's a gift from God.

"For it is by grace you have been saved, through faith - and this not from yourselves, it is the gift of God..." Ephesians 2:8

"And we know that in all things God works for the good of those who love him, who have been called according to his purpose."
Romans 8:28

Failures produce successes.

Peace has an enemy. Striving.

"There remains, then, a Sabbath-rest for the people of
God; for anyone who enters God's rest also rests from
his own work, just as God did from his."
Hebrews 4:9-10

"Sow your seed in the morning, and at evening let not your hands be idle, for you do not know which will succeed, whether this or that, or whether both will do equally well."
Ecclesiastes 11:6

It's ok to say
'I don't know'

'Slow down, you're going too fast'. Busyness can be your worst enemy.

"Be still, and know that I am God; I will be exalted among the nations..." Psalm 46:10

Integrity is what happens in you

"May integrity and uprightness protect me,
because my hope is in you." Psalm 25:21

not to you.

The presence of God doesn't

exclude you from failure.

Our failure is not a problem to God. Our pride is.

"God opposes the proud but gives grace to the humble." James 4:6

'Paying consequences' is a wonderful teacher.

"When he came to his senses, he said,
'How many of my father's hired men have food to spare,
and here I am starving to death!" Luke 15:17

mercy

wisdom

intimacy

faith

the cornerstones

Paul said
'I have learned ...'
not 'I have been taught'.
Become a learner today.

"I am not saying this because I am in need, for I have
learned to be content whatever the circumstances. I know
what it is to be in need, and I know what it is to have
plenty. I have learned the secret of being content in any
and every situation, whether well fed or hungry, whether
living in plenty or in want. I can do everything through
him who gives me strength." Philippians 4:11-13

"...faith comes from hearing the message, and the message is heard through the word of Christ." Romans 10:17

Live by what God has said yet be led by what God is saying.

Having no experience can be to your advantage.
Never let experience replace learning and listening.

"He said, "Throw your net on the right side of the boat and you will find some." When they did, they were unable to haul the net in because of the large number of fish." John 21:6

God doesn't bless hard work.

He blesses commanded work.

Don't worry what people think
Rejoice with what heaven knows.

"Before I formed you in the womb I knew
you, before you were born I set you apart; I
appointed you as a prophet to the nations."
Jeremiah 1:5

"I have been crucified with Christ and I no longer live, but Christ lives in me. The life I live in the body, I live by faith in the Son of God, who loved me and gave himself for me.."
Galatians 2:20

The enemy to God's development in your life is self-development.

"He who has an ear, let him hear
what the Spirit says to the churches.
To him who overcomes, I will give
the right to eat from the tree of life,
which is in the paradise of God."
Revelation 2:7

It's time to lead with our ears.

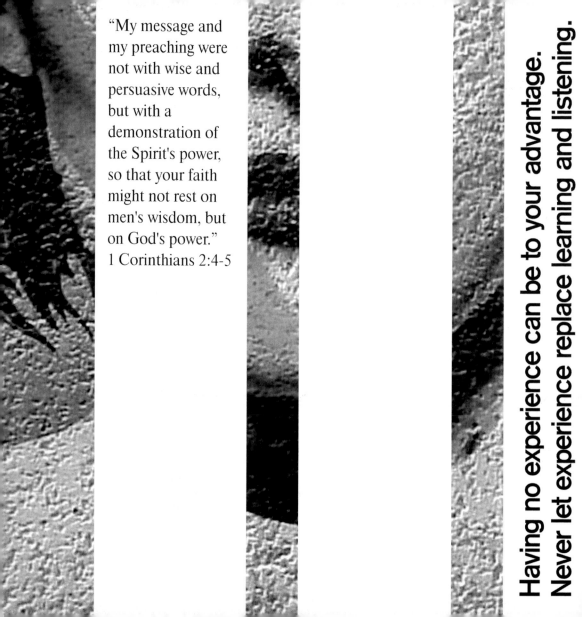

"My message and my preaching were not with wise and persuasive words, but with a demonstration of the Spirit's power, so that your faith might not rest on men's wisdom, but on God's power."
1 Corinthians 2:4-5

Having no experience can be to your advantage.
Never let experience replace learning and listening.

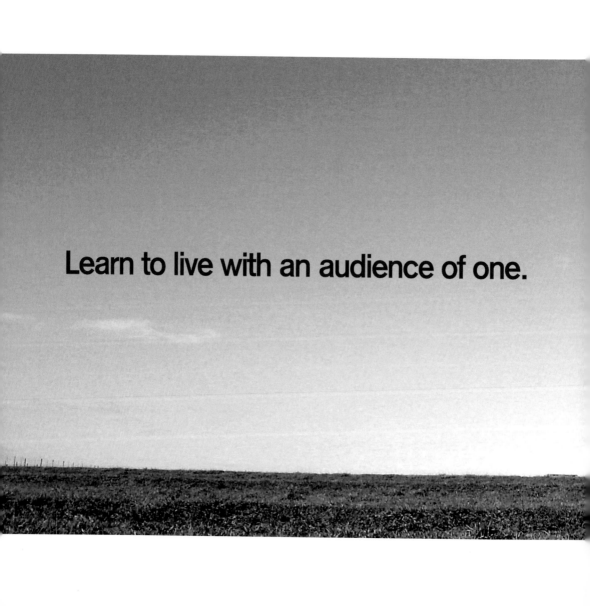

"Jesus called out with a loud voice, "Father, into your hands I commit my spirit."
When he had said this, he breathed his last." Luke 23:46

"This is the confidence we have in approaching God: that if we ask anything according to his will, he hears us. And if we know that he hears us - whatever we ask - we know that we have what we asked of him." 1 John 5:14-15

Heaven may be silent but it's not deaf.

"I am the vine; you are the branches. If a man remains in me and I in him, he will bear much fruit; apart from me you can do nothing." John 15:5

It's time to lose your worn out religious traditions
It's time to become predictably unpredictable

When water is still it becomes clear.
Learn to still your life.

Stillness is an uncluttered spirit.

The Holy Spirit doesn't apologise for the humanity of the people He uses.

mercy

wisdom

intimacy

faith

the cornerstones

Trust is faith plus nothing.

"Have faith in God," Jesus answered. "I tell you the truth, if anyone says to this mountain, 'Go, throw yourself into the sea,' and does not doubt in his heart but believes that what he says will happen, it will be done for him." Mark 11:22-23

God is always doing something new.

See, I am doing a new thing! Now it springs up; do you not perceive it? I am making a way in the desert and streams in the wasteland." Isaiah 43:19

Samson said, "Give me one more crack at this."
That's the spirit!

"O Sovereign LORD,
remember me. O God,
please strengthen me just
once more, and let me with
one blow get revenge on
the Philistines for my two
eyes." Judges 16:28

Don't be afraid of showing
the dead areas of your life
because there's honey
in them.

Judges 14:5-9

"...being confident of this, that He who began a good work in you will carry it on to completion until the day of Christ Jesus."

Philippians 1:6

My confidence is
His confidence in me to do it.

Jesus didn't respond to every touch.

Nor should you.

"And those he predestined, he also called; those he called, he also justified; those he justified, he also glorified." Romans 8:30

Destiny is not a patch
It's a quilt.

God is the greatest recycler on the planet.

"Restore to me the joy of your salvation and grant me a willing spirit, to sustain me." Psalm 51:12

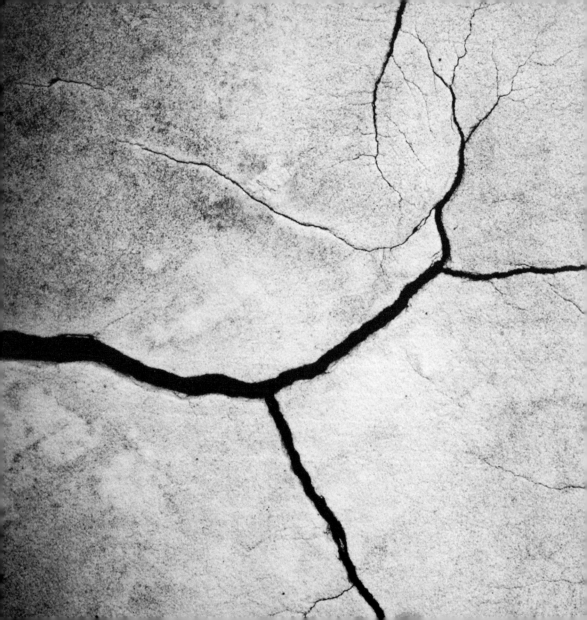

God uses broken vessels.

"But we have this treasure in jars of clay to show that this all-surpassing power is from God and not from us."
2 Corinthians 4:7

"They will rebuild the ancient ruins and restore the places long devastated; they will renew the ruined cities that have been devastated for generations." Isaiah 61:4

also available in

the **DEVOTIONAL RESCUE** series

the **DEVOTIONAL RESCUE** series

Heaven Sent
Wisdom from the Father's Heart

DAVE & JENNY GILPIN

the **DEVOTIONAL RESCUE** series

Classic Lines
Devotional Insights for Women

JENNY GILPIN

the **DEVOTIONAL RESCUE** series

IT'S TIME TO LEAVE THE
Cemetery
PAST HURTS

REPOSITIONING YOUR LIFE FOR THE NEXT BIG THING!
RAY BEVAN